The Anti-Inflammatory Mediterranean Diet Revolution

Eddison .H Robles

Introduction

This book provides readers with a comprehensive guide to understanding and implementing an anti-inflammatory diet, with a focus on Mediterranean cuisine. The book covers various aspects of this dietary approach, helping beginners make informed choices for a healthier lifestyle.

The book begins by explaining the concept of inflammation and its significance in the context of health. It introduces readers to the anti-inflammatory diet and its basic principles, including the role of carbohydrates, fats, and proteins in this dietary approach.

Readers are then introduced to five key types of anti-inflammatory foods that they should incorporate into their diet. These include vegetables, especially cruciferous vegetables, fibrous foods like legumes, fruits, herbs, and spices such as turmeric, ginger, cinnamon, and garlic, and lean proteins, with a focus on fish.

The book also highlights inflammatory foods that individuals should limit or avoid, such as refined sugars, processed and ultra-processed foods, refined grains, and trans fats. A detailed food list is provided to help readers make informed choices when planning their meals.

A 7-day sample menu is included to assist beginners in getting started with their anti-inflammatory diet. This practical example offers a glimpse into what a week of anti-inflammatory eating might look like.

The book discusses the potential health benefits of following an anti-inflammatory diet, emphasizing how it can positively impact overall well-being. It also addresses any potential disadvantages of this dietary approach.

Readers are given insights into what to expect when starting the anti-inflammatory diet, helping them prepare for the changes they may experience as they adopt this healthier eating pattern.

The book then delves into the Mediterranean diet, offering information about its key components, including vegetables, fruits, whole grains, pulses, healthy fats, fish, herbs, and spices. It also outlines foods to be eaten in moderation and those to limit.

To further assist beginners, the book presents ten essential facts about the Mediterranean diet, summarizing its core principles and benefits.

The book concludes with a section on anti-inflammatory diet recipes, providing readers with practical ideas for incorporating these dietary principles into their daily meals.

Overall, this book offers a comprehensive and informative guide to adopting a healthy eating pattern that can help reduce inflammation and promote well-being. It equips readers with the knowledge and tools needed to get started on their journey toward a healthier lifestyle.

Contents

Inflammation, explained

When working to understand the link between chronic inflammation and chronic disease, Shayna Komar, RD, a Licensed and Registered Oncology Dietitian with Cancer Wellness of Piedmont Hospital in Atlanta, Georgia, suggests that we start by defining the two types of inflammation: acute and chronic.

Komar explains, "Inflammation is sometimes confusing, because it may seem contradictory. On one hand, inflammation is a healthy process, allowing the body's ability to heal itself. When you have an infection or injury, the immune system releases white blood cells and chemicals to fight off the infection or repair damaged tissue." This type of inflammation is called acute inflammation, and it is helpful to the body.

Inflammation may become dangerous when it persists, even at low levels, for extended periods of time. Carolyn Williams, PhD RD, a registered dietitian and author of the anti-inflammatory cookbook, Meals that Heal, shares, "Chronic inflammation is like a small fire burning inside the body that, over time, gets stoked and encouraged by other irritants, taking a gradual toll on the body by damaging cells, overworking the immune system and creating imbalance that can lead to long-term health issues."

Komar agrees, "When you don't have an infection or injury, inflammation can potentially damage healthy tissues. Chronic, low-grade inflammation is inflammation that never really resolves. It's the opposite of 'good' inflammation and may actually damage DNA."

This is particularly troublesome to those who are undergoing treatment for a chronic condition, as the underlying chronic inflammation potentially fuels the disease.

The positive news is that many of these risk factors for developing chronic inflammation and chronic disease are within our control. One of the easiest and most readily accessible ways that we can reduce inflammation is through eating a diet high in anti-inflammatory foods.

What is the anti-inflammatory diet?

Fresh Fruits and Vegetables

When looking for ways to keep chronic inflammation at bay, research consistently points to four key lifestyle factors: including exercise, reducing stress, managing weight, and getting proper nutrition. When it comes to nutrition and inflammation, this means including anti-inflammatory foods and excluding inflammatory foods.

Komar provides clarity on the role of anti-inflammatory foods, saying, "Certain food components can affect inflammation pathways in your body." She echoes Williams' statement and shares, "It is like a fire: What you eat can either put 'fuel' to the fire by eating many foods that cause inflammation or you can stop the fire by following an anti-inflammatory diet and lifestyle."

The anti-inflammatory diet takes principals from the Mediterranean diet, studied since the 1960s, and the DASH diet (Dietary Approaches to Stop Hypertension), developed in the 1990s, and has been attributed to Andrew Weil, MD, Harvard University graduate and founder of the Center for Integrative Medicine at the University of Arizona. Weil introduced the anti-inflammatory diet, including an anti-inflammatory food pyramid, in Eating Well for Optimum Health, published in 2000.

The principals of the anti-inflammatory diet are still very relevant today and have increasingly gained popularity over the last 20 years, as studies continue to support the theory that diet can reduce chronic inflammation and can reduce or prevent the instance of chronic disease.

Basic principals of the anti-inflammatory diet

Though the anti-inflammatory diet is not a calorie-restrictive diet, its emphasis on whole, unprocessed foods and reduced sugars and flours may result in weight loss.

The guidelines suggest consuming between 2,000 to 3,000 calories each day depending on gender and activity level with men and more active people needing more calories, and women and less active people needing less calories.

The anti-inflammatory diet recommends that 40 to 50 percent of daily calories come from carbohydrates, 30 percent from fat and 20 to 30 percent from protein; with an emphasis on including carbohydrates, fat, and protein in every meal.

Carbohydrates

Vegetables and fruits should make up most of the carbohydrates consumed daily on the anti-inflammatory diet. Beans and whole grains (not whole wheat flour) can also be consumed to add bulk and satiety in this category.

Fats

Avocado Prices Are Nearly Double What They Were This Time Last Year
Monounsaturated fats like extra-virgin olive oil, nuts, avocados, and seeds are the healthy fats to be enjoyed on the anti-inflammatory diet. Saturated fats, including animal fats and fats that are solid at room temperature, should be used sparingly. Polyunsaturated fats include omega-6 and omega-3 fatty acids and fats that remain liquid at room temperature; focus on including omega-3 fatty acids from this category.

Proteins

An emphasis on plant-based and lean protein is recommended on the anti-inflammatory diet. Beans, particularly soybeans and whole soy products, and fish, especially fish high in omega-3 fatty acids, are recommended. Limit animal protein and avoid red meat.

In addition, the anti-inflammatory diet suggests that the timing of your meals is important. Dr. Weil recommends that calories be consumed within an 11-hour window, leaving 13 hours overnight as a "fasting period." He suggests that this fasting period provides time for the body to recalibrate immunity, repair cells, and replenish its capacity for antioxidants.

Five types of anti-inflammatory foods to eat

It is important to look at the overall diet you consume instead of focusing on individual foods. Komar encourages her patients to look at nutrition as a part of their treatment plan.

Research indicates that by consistently focusing on a healthy diet pattern, you can reduce inflammation. Komar shares, "It is all about focusing on your pattern of eating as opposed to choosing a few particular foods to reduce inflammation."
With this in mind, we look at five categories of foods essential to the anti-inflammatory diet, and the properties of each that are backed by research and by experts in the field.

Vegetables especially cruciferous vegetables

Leaves of raw kale weight loss foods nutritionists
Veggies provide nutrients that are vital to fighting inflammation and maintaining proper body function. Packed with vitamins and minerals, veggies are also an excellent source of fiber.

Cabbage, cauliflower, broccoli, Brussels sprouts, kale, arugula, collard greens, and even wasabi are just a few of the varieties in a group of plants called cruciferous vegetables. These veggies are recognizable for their pungent odor and sometimes bitter flavor and are often touted for their anti-cancer properties. These nutrient-rich veggies contain carotenoids, a type of antioxidant, vitamin C, E, K, folate, minerals, and fiber.

Fibrous foods especially legumes

A staple of the Mediterranean and the anti-inflammatory diet, legumes are a category of vegetables that includes beans, peas, and lentils. Legumes provide some of the highest natural sources of fiber found in any food and also provide an excellent source of plant-based protein.

Fiber is key to reducing inflammation, and the consumption of legumes has been shown to have an impact on the body's immune function. A diet high in fiber has even been found to protect against certain cancers, including breast cancer.

Fruit especially berries

Fruit is nature's candy. Whereas refined sugar is inflammatory and should be avoided on the anti-inflammatory diet, fruit is anti-inflammatory. It helps provide much-needed energy by giving a boost of natural sugar—and you don't get the sugar crash of a refined sugar product because fruit contains fiber, which slows down the metabolic process and stabilizes blood sugar.

Of all the beautiful fruits available to us, berries are the star of the show to reduce inflammation. Blueberries, strawberries, blackberries, and raspberries are high in antioxidants and are just a few of the many berries that are suggested as part of an anti-inflammatory diet. Additionally, the anthocyanins that produce berries' beautiful colors are also a powerful phytochemical that may provide anti-inflammatory properties.

Herbs and Spices especially turmeric, ginger, cinnamon, and garlic

Turmeric

Often overlooked as a source of nutrition, herbs and spices provide excellent anti-inflammatory properties. In addition to eating a wide variety of veggies and fruits, Komar shares, "It is also important to incorporate herbs and spices such as turmeric, garlic, ginger, and cinnamon to help decrease inflammation."

Turmeric is a major source of curcumin, a micro-nutrient that has long been known for its antioxidant and anti-inflammatory properties. When adding turmeric to recipes, also add a pinch of black pepper to boost absorption of curcumin.

Ginger is a root that can reduce inflammation and pain, making it extremely helpful to those working to reduce chronic inflammation. Studies have also found that consuming ginger helps alleviate the nausea and vomiting that many patients experience during chemotherapy treatments for cancer.

Cinnamon is a spice that has been commonly used since 2800 BC. It is being studied for its potential in cancer therapy and has been shown to have anti-oxidant and anti-inflammatory properties.

Garlic isn't just a delicious way to add depth of flavor to your dishes, it's a rich source of selenium with sulfur-containing compounds that are being studied for their possible effect on carcinogens.

Lean protein especially fish

Protein is vital to the formation, maintenance, and repair of body tissues. Ensuring that you get an adequate amount of protein in your daily diet is especially important as we age in order to maintain muscle mass.

In addition to being an excellent source of lean protein, fatty fish is also high in omega-3 fatty acids, which are essential to lowering inflammation. Fatty seafood like salmon, trout, albacore tuna, Atlantic herring, Atlantic mackerel, anchovies, sardines, and even mussels, provide an excellent dietary source of omega-threes and lean protein.

Inflammatory foods to limit

It is typically best to adopt a positive mindset of including as many anti-inflammatory, whole foods as possible in your diet to weed out the inflammatory foods. But it's also helpful to recognize the foods that are the biggest contributors to inflammation limit them in your everyday diet.

Refined sugars

Natural sugars found in fruit are not inflammatory in nature. However, when we look at refined sugars, the story is different. Refined sugars include cane sugar, granulated sugar, powdered sugar, brown sugar, high fructose corn syrup... the list goes on.

With no nutrients or fiber to slow down the absorption process, these products offer little to no nutritional value, and consumption of refined sugars has been associated with increased inflammation leading to higher instances of heart disease, diabetes, cancer, and cognitive decline. Look at labels when purchasing packaged foods manufacturers often sneak in added sugar to make products more shelf-stable.

Processed and ultra-processed foods

The more a food transforms from its original source before you eat it, the more likely it is to cause inflammation. A recent study found that a higher intake of ultra-processed foods was associated with a higher risk of inflammatory bowel disease.

The majority of packaged foods, fast foods, and industrially-created ingredients are processed or ultra-processed. Avoid the worst of these by reading labels and choosing foods with the lowest number of ingredients (ingredients you know and can pronounce and that do not include added sugar).

Additionally, there is a link between ultra-processed foods and sugars: Ultra-processed foods make up 90% of the added sugars that Americans consume. If you cut out the ultra-processed foods, you go a long way in cutting out the added sugar.

Refined grains

While whole grains are recommended for their anti-inflammatory properties, research shows that the intake of refined grains is associated with pro-inflammatory effects.

Avoid foods or goods made with white flour, white rice, and pasta and scan labels for the word "enriched." If an item has been "enriched," it means that nutrients were taken out in processing and then added back in during production. This signals a refined grain product and should be avoided.

Trans fats

Trans fats are oils that have been altered chemically during processing and studies indicate that they are directly linked to systemic inflammation in women.
Fast foods, fried foods, packaged snacks, bakery goods, shortening, and margarine are common sources of trans fats. Additionally, packaged foods with ingredients shown as "hydrogenated" or "partially-hydrogenated" are indicators that the food contains trans fats.

A Food List of What to Eat and Avoid on an Anti-Inflammatory Diet

Following an anti-inflammatory diet means loading up on foods that research has shown can help lower inflammation and reducing your intake of foods that have the opposite effect. One of the best things about the diet is that there are plenty of food options and lots of wiggle room, so you can pick and choose the foods you like best.

If you need a little more structure, consider adopting the Mediterranean diet. There's a lot of overlap with the anti-inflammatory diet because both emphasize eating fruits, vegetables, and whole grains.

Anti-Inflammatory Foods to Eat

- Fresh fruit, including grapefruit, grapes, blueberries, bananas, apples, mangoes, peaches, tomatoes, and pomegranates
- Dried fruit, including plums (prunes)
- Vegetables, especially broccoli, Brussels sprouts, cauliflower, and bok choy
- Plant-based proteins, such as chickpeas, seitan, and lentils
- Fatty fish, such as salmon, sardines, albacore tuna, herring, lake trout, and mackerel
- Whole grains, including oatmeal, brown rice, barley, and whole-wheat bread
- Leafy greens, including kale, spinach, and romaine lettuce
- Ginger
- Nuts, including walnuts and almonds
- Seeds, such as chia seeds and flaxseed
- Foods filled with omega-3 fatty acids, such as avocado and olive oil
- Coffee
- Green tea
- Dark chocolate (in moderation)
- Red wine (in moderation)

Foods to Eat Sparingly or Avoid to Help Avoid Inflammation

- Refined carbohydrates, such as white bread, pastries, and sweets
- Foods and drinks that are high in sugar, including soda and other sugary beverages
- Red meat
- Dairy

- Processed meat, such as hot dogs and sausages
- Fried foods

A 7-Day Sample Menu for Anti-Inflammatory Diet Beginners

The following sample menu isn't one-size-fits-all, but it does offer some creative ideas for adding anti-inflammatory foods to your meals. If you're managing a certain disease, such as diabetes, you may have dietary needs that this meal plan doesn't address. Be sure to consult your healthcare team before making any major changes to your eating habits.

Day 1

Breakfast Steel-cut oats with slivered almonds and blueberries and a cup of coffee

Lunch Chopped kale salad with chickpeas, beets, and pomegranate seeds tossed with an olive oil and lemon juice vinaigrette

Dinner Anchovy, salmon, and tomato-topped pizza on a cauliflower crust

Snack Small handful of homemade trail mix with unsalted nuts and raisins

Day 2

Breakfast Steel-cut oatmeal topped with walnuts and sliced strawberries; a cup of coffee

Lunch Salmon sashimi with a side of broccoli and a side of brown rice and ginger

Dinner Ginger curry with whitefish, kale, barley, and a glass of red wine

Snack Sliced mango

Day 3

Breakfast Quinoa bowl with sliced banana, blueberries, and a drizzle of almond butter; a cup of green tea

Lunch Arugula salad with albacore tuna, grilled peaches, and walnuts
Dinner Spinach salad with grilled salmon and a side of brown rice

Snack Frozen grapes

Day 4

Breakfast Kale and mushroom frittata, half a grapefruit, and a cup of coffee

Lunch Grain bowl with brown rice, chickpeas, and sautéed bok choy

Dinner Veggie burger on a whole-grain bun with a side of roasted Brussels sprouts

Snack Small handful of unsalted mixed nuts.

Day 5

Breakfast Chia seed pudding, apple slices with almond butter, and a cup of green tea

Lunch Spinach salad with tuna and shredded carrots

Dinner Red peppers stuffed with ground turkey, quinoa, chickpeas, and a glass of red wine

Snack Small handful of unsalted almonds

Day 6

Breakfast Soy yogurt with fresh blueberries and a cup of coffee

Lunch Quinoa bowl with sardines, tomatoes, black beans, sautéed spinach, and avocado

Dinner Salmon with lentils and a spinach salad

Snack A square of dark chocolate and a small handful of unsalted mixed nuts

Day 7

Breakfast Peanut butter and banana sandwich and a cup of coffee

Lunch Smashed avocado and halved cherry tomatoes on top of whole-grain toast, and a side of cottage cheese

Dinner Seitan with bell peppers, mushrooms, and broccoli stir-fried in olive oil

What Are the Possible Health Benefits of Following an Anti-Inflammatory Diet?

Following an anti-inflammatory diet has been shown to help people with:

- Autoimmune disorders including RA and MS
- Heart disease
- Cancer, including breast cancer and colorectal cancer
- Alzheimer's disease
- Diabetes
- Pulmonary disease
- Epilepsy

Are There Any Disadvantages to an Anti-Inflammatory Diet?

There are no major downsides associated with the anti-inflammatory diet though there may be a learning curve to master which inflammation-fighting foods to eat and which foods to avoid.

If your diet is currently filled with processed foods, meat, and dairy, you may have a bit of an adjustment period. You'll want to clear your fridge and pantry of potentially inflammatory foods, and you'll likely need to devote more time and effort to meal prep, since stopping for fast food is a no-go on this diet.

What to Expect When You Start the Anti-Inflammatory Diet

Once you start eating this way, you'll probably start to feel better overall. "People may feel better, with less bloating, gastrointestinal discomfort, and achiness," Scanniello says. You may also see your mood improve as you change your eating habits.

But don't expect to notice immediate changes with regard to a health condition it'll likely take two or three weeks for you to notice that kind of effect, and possibly up to 12 weeks to know whether the results will stick, according to the American Osteopathic Association's website The DO

What is the Mediterranean Diet?

This way of eating focuses on foods like olive oil, nuts, fruits and vegetables, legumes, whole grains and fish. Wine is part of the typical Mediterranean diet, too, but you should drink it in moderation. This style of diet can also include some dairy and poultry ingredients but, like wine, these are usually limited.

The Mediterranean diet places an emphasis on fresh, colorful eating and shuns heavily processed ingredients. Trust us, your plate will never be boring. Even better news: though "diet" is in the name, this plan is more of a holistic approach to eating that relies on real foods. You won't be counting calories or macronutrients like you would with a typical "diet."

Here are three reasons to make space on your plate for Mediterranean diet foods.
It can keep your heart healthier

In a 2013 study in the New England Journal of Medicine, researchers found that people on a Mediterranean diet were far less likely to have a heart attack, stroke or other cardiovascular event than people who ate a low-fat diet. The study participants who ate a Mediterranean diet supplemented with olive oil or nuts saw their risk of cardiovascular disease drop by 30 percent.

It can have weight-loss benefits

In a study on younger women, those who most closely followed a Mediterranean diet had a lower body mass index (BMI) and smaller waist and thighs than those who adhered to the diet's style the least. This is likely because the diet is high in antioxidants and provides rich anti-inflammatory properties. It's also packed with fiber, a nutrient known for keeping you full.

It can support better brain health

A 2016 review of 18 studies in Frontiers in Nutrition found that eating Mediterranean was associated with less cognitive decline, reduced risk of Alzheimer's disease, and better memory and executive function. Additional research in the journal Neurology likened the diet's effects to reducing the brain's age by five years.

Mediterranean Diet Food List: How to Follow This Popular Meal Plan

For the fifth year in a row, the Mediterranean diet won best overall diet in the US News & World Report's annual ranking, and there's a reason why: Research has linked the popular way of eating to a longer lifespan and a lower risk of type 2 diabetes, heart disease, and age-related memory decline.

Unlike other popular diets, the Mediterranean diet doesn't involve strict rules like calorie counting or macro tracking. Instead, followers consume foods that are part of the traditional diet of people who live in countries bordering the Mediterranean Sea lots of vegetables, whole grains, healthy fats, and fish. If this sounds like an eating style for you, here's an overview of the specific foods that make up the bulk of the Mediterranean diet, plus the foods you should limit.

Vegetables and Fruits

People who follow the Mediterranean diet eat four or more servings of vegetables a day and three or more servings of fruit, making produce a key staple. For reference, only 10% of American adults eat the recommended two to three cups of vegetables daily and just 12.3% eat the advised one and a half to two cups of fruit, according to the Centers for Disease Control and Prevention (CDC).

Produce consumed on a Mediterranean diet includes:

- Artichokes
- Beets
- Broccoli
- Brussels sprouts
- Cabbage
- Carrots

- Celery
- Cucumbers
- Eggplant
- Leafy Greens
- Mushrooms
- Onions
- Peppers
- Potatoes
- Sweet Potatoes
- Tomatoes
- Zucchini
- Apples
- Apricots
- Berries
- Cherries
- Citrus
- Dates
- Figs
- Grapes
- Melons
- Peaches
- Pears
- Pomegranates

The vitamins, minerals, fiber, and antioxidants found in these fruits and veggies can help reduce your risk of heart disease and cancer (the two leading causes of death in the US), and they may also boost your mental health. A 2020 study in the journal Nutrients also found that adults who consumed at least five servings of produce per day saw improvement in general well-being, sleep quality, life satisfaction, mood, curiosity, creativity, optimism, self-esteem, and happiness—not to mention a reduction in stress, nervousness, and anxiety.

While that all sounds great, it can be overwhelming trying to eat that much produce in a 24-hour period. My tip? When deciding what to eat for a meal or snack, start with produce first. Whip leafy greens and fruit into a breakfast smoothie. Swap a lunchtime sandwich for an entree salad, and replace half your dinner portion of pasta with spiralized zucchini or any vegetable. Round out the day with snacks like fruits and nuts or veggies with hummus.

Whole Grains

People in the Mediterranean region tend to consume three to four servings of whole grains daily, with one serving equal to a half cup of cooked whole grain or slice of bread. Whole grains found in a Mediterranean diet include:

- Barley
- Buckwheat
- Corn
- Millet
- Oats
- Whole wheat
- Whole grain bread
- Whole grain pasta
- Whole grain rice

Even though Americans are eating more whole grains, less than 16% of total daily grain consumption comes from whole grains, according to the CDC. This is concerning, given a 2018 review published in the European Journal of Clinical Nutrition found that high consumption of whole grains was associated with a lower risk of heart disease, cancer, and overall death.

Try upgrading your refined grains to their whole counterparts. For example, swap a breakfast pastry for a bowl of oatmeal; opt for brown rice over white at dinner, or replace your white bread sandwich for a lunchtime salad made with cooked quinoa.

Pulses

Pulses include all varieties of beans, lentils, peas, and chickpeas. On the Mediterranean diet, three or more servings of pulses are consumed per week, and for good reason: A 2021 study published in Nutrients found that people who consumed pulses also had higher intakes of fiber, folate, and magnesium compared to those who didn't eat pulses. Those who consumed 2.5 ounces roughly a half cup of cooked chickpeas or other pulses also got more potassium, zinc, iron, and choline, along with lower amounts of fat.

Commonly eaten pulses in the Mediterranean diet include:

- Cannellini beans
- Chickpeas
- Fava beans
- Kidney beans
- Lentils
- Split peas

If you're wondering how to incorporate more pulses into your diet, simply swap them in for meat. For example, instead of beef stew, try lentil soup. Or, snack on roasted chickpeas over beef jerky.

Healthy Fats

In the Mediterranean, people consume so much olive oil about four tablespoons daily that it's practically its own food group. While fat can get a bad rep, the healthy fats found in olive oil are important for our health. A 2019 report published in Nutrients stated, "extra virgin olive oil (EVOO) should, indeed, be the fat of choice when it comes to human health." Why? Because EVOO consumption is linked with lower incidences of heart disease, cancer, high blood pressure, autoimmune diseases, and inflammatory conditions, like ulcerative colitis.

Other healthful Mediterranean fats include avocado (technically a fruit, but still chock full of good fat) as well as nuts and seeds. In fact, you should eat nuts or seeds at least three times per week on the diet. For reference, a serving size would be 1/4 cup of nuts or two tablespoons of nut or seed butter. Common nuts consumed in the diet include:

- Almonds
- Cashews
- Hazelnuts
- Olives
- Pine nuts
- Pistachios
- Sesame seeds
- Tahini
- Walnuts

Work these healthy fats into daily meals and snacks by blending nut butter or avocado into smoothies; dressing salads with EVOO and balsamic vinaigrette; and sauteeing veggies in EVOO instead of butter.

Fish

People following a traditional Mediterranean diet eat three to four ounces of fish about three times per week. The types of fish consumed include those rich in anti-inflammatory omega-3 fatty acids, like sardines, salmon, and mackerel. Other types of seafood to eat:

- Clams

- Crab
- Eel
- Flounder
- Herring
- Lobster
- Mussels
- Octopus
- Oysters
- Sea bass
- Shrimp
- Tuna

Research indicates eating fish can prolong not only the quantity but quality of life. A 2020 analysis in Nutrients found that for every additional 20 grams of fish consumed per day about ¼ of a three-ounce salmon filet the risk of dying from cardiovascular disease decreased by 4%.

Additionally, a 2018 study published in the American Journal of Epidemiology found that a higher fish intake was associated with decreased rates of cognitive decline in older adults. This was particularly true for episodic memory a type of long-term memory that involves recalling previous experiences with their context, in terms of time, place, and emotions.

Herbs and Spices

Natural seasonings are a vital part of a Mediterranean diet because they offer not only aroma, color, and flavor, but also added nutrients and health benefits. According to a 2019 review published in the Journal of AOAC International, herbs and spices possess antioxidant, anti-inflammatory, and anti-cancer properties. They also lower blood sugar and cholesterol levels as well as positively impact mood, cognition, and the gut microbiome.

Herbs and spices used liberally in a Mediterranean eating plan include:

- Anise Basil Bay Leaf
- Chiles Cloves Cumin
- Garlic Lavender Marjoram
- Mint Oregano Parsley
- Pepper Rosemary Sage
- Sumac Tarragon Thyme

Have fun experimenting with herbs and spices by adding fresh mint to a smoothie or hot tea; infusing water with fresh herbs and fruit; or whisking garlic and herbs with oil and vinegar to make a simple homemade vinaigrette.

Foods To Eat In Moderation on the Mediterranean Diet

The food groups above make up the foundation of a Mediterranean Diet. But the eating plan also includes moderate portions of poultry, eggs, and dairy (especially fermented dairy like Greek yogurt and kefir). So what does moderate mean? That varies depending on your personal preference. You might choose to consume very small portions of dairy daily or eat larger amounts on a weekly basis.

Although optional, red wine is traditionally enjoyed daily by Mediterranean eaters. Just stick to one 5-ounce glass per day if you're a woman and no more than two glasses per day if you are a man, according to the Dietary Guidelines for Americans 2020-2025.

Foods To Limit on a Mediterranean Diet

While the Mediterranean diet doesn't require you to cut out one food group or food entirely, it does encourage people to limit or avoid these items:

- Red meat. Consumed regularly in small amounts, it can increase the risk of colorectal cancer, according to the American Institute of Cancer Research (AICR).
- Sweets. In excess, they boost the risk of obesity, type 2 diabetes, heart disease, Alzheimer's disease, high blood pressure, and more, according to the American Heart Association.
- Highly processed foods. According to a 2021 study in the journal Nutrients, each 10% increase in calories from highly processed food was associated with a 15% higher risk of death from all causes.

Specific examples of foods to limit on a Mediterranean Diet include:

- Alcohol, other than red wine in moderation
- Bacon
- Candy
- Commercial baked goods
- Fast food
- Frozen pizza
- Ham
- Hotdogs
- Lunch meat
- Pepperoni
- Processed cheese
- Refined oils
- Sausage
- Soda and sugary drinks

- White bread
- White pasta
- White rice

Simple swaps can help curb your intake of these foods. For example, try trading soda for sparkling water; vegetables in place of pepperoni and sausage on pizza; or eating low-sodium canned soups instead of fast food when you're in a hurry.

10 Things to Know About the Mediterranean Diet

Eating this diet, which is rich in fruits and vegetables, healthy fats, and whole grains, can lower your risk for certain health problems. Here are a few ways you can improve your health by eating the Mediterranean Diet.

1. Pile on fruit and vegetables

Fresh, non-starchy produce is the star of this diet. Eat 5 to 10 servings a day (a half-cup cooked or 1 cup raw equals one serving).

2. Choose healthy fats

Olives and their oil are cornerstones; go for four to six servings per day (a serving could be 1 tsp. of olive oil, 5 olives or 1/8 of an avocado). Olive oil delivers healthy monounsaturated fats and plant compounds called polyphenols.

3. Pick seeds, nuts, and legume

The star of the bowl, acai, is a superfood that's bursting with antioxidants, and may also have weight loss and anti-aging benefits.

4. Focus on fish and eggs

Make these individual veggie frittatas on Sunday night for an easy, low-calorie breakfast you can eat during the week. Super simple to make, you can also change up the vegetables to suit the season (or what you have in the fridge).

5. Do have (some) dairy

Here's a healthy treat you can serve at your next BBQ and the preparation is easier than (peach) pie. Simply grill peach halves, top with honey and Greek yogurt, and serve. Watch the video for a step-by-step demonstration.

6. Get grain-wise

Refined carbs lack nutrients and can wreak havoc on your blood sugar. Whole grains are best; have four small daily portions of whole-wheat bread, or try a pasta made from quinoa. And always eat grains with healthy fats and protein. Incorporate sprouted or fermented grains (hello, sourdough!) for easier digestion and better nutrient absorption. Or look for creative ways to swap out grains, such as using spaghetti squash in place of noodles.

7. Add herbs and spices

When the weather is chilly or when you just don't feel like whipping up dinner after a long day of work, this slow-cooker chicken recipe is a lifesaver.

8. Rethink what you drink

Are you drinking enough water each day? With these tips from Holley Grainger, RD, filling up on the recommended 13 to 16 cups is easier than you think. Watch this Cooking Light video to learn more.

9. Eat locally

One of the best strategies for healthy, sustainable eating is choosing fresh, local ingredients. But as we all know, it can be challenging to locate in-season produce from nearby growers without putting in some major effort. That's why Natalie Chanin, founder of the sustainable lifestyle and clothing company Alabama Chanin took it upon herself to provide local foods to her community.

10. Make it social

Relaxed meals with family and friends are a core part of life in this region. This positive attitude toward eating helps improve digestion and lower stress, too.

Anti-inflammatory Diet Recipes

Cherry Quinoa Breakfast

Ingredients:
½ cup dried quinoa
½ tsp. vanilla
¼ tsp. cinnamon
½ cup dried unsweetened cherries
1 cup water

Directions:
Prepare the porridge in a medium saucepan. Add water, dried quinoa, unsweetened cherries, vanilla, and cinnamon to the saucepan and bring them to a simmer. Once the concoction simmers, reduce the heat. Allow it to simmer for fifteen minutes. All of the water should disappear. Serve the porridge hot for a satisfying, anti-inflammatory breakfast.

Cinnamon Ginger Oatmeal

Ingredients:
1 cup water
½ cup oats
¼ cup dried cranberries
1 tsp. ground ginger
½ tsp. ground cinnamon
¼ tsp. ground nutmeg
1 tbsp. flaxseed
1 tbsp. molasses

Directions:
Bring the oats, water, dried cranberries, ginger, cinnamon, and nutmeg to a boil in a medium-sized saucepan. When the mixture

begins to boil, turn down the heat and allow it to simmer for five minutes. Afterwards, add your flaxseeds. Cover the pan for five minutes and allow the mixture to assimilate. Serve warm.

No-Wheat Morning Granola

Ingredients:
3 tbsp. honey
3 tbsp. coconut oil
1 tsp. vanilla
¼ tsp. cinnamon
¼ tsp. ginger
1 cup buckwheat groats
1 cup cooked quinoa
½ cup oats
½ cup unsweetened cranberries

Directions:

Begin by preheating your oven to 325 degrees Fahrenheit. Prepare your baking sheet with light grease.

Next, stir together honey, coconut oil, vanilla, cinnamon, and ginger. Set aside. In a larger bowl, stir together your buckwheat groats, quinoa, and oats. Next, add your small bowl to your big bowl and stir.

Spread the mixture into a solid layer on the baking sheet. Bake the mixture for 45 minutes. Your grains should begin to brown. Afterwards, stir in your cranberries. Allow the granola to cool prior to storing. Be sure to serve with almond milk or rice milk!

Spinach Garlic Frittata

Ingredients:
1 pound sliced mushrooms
1 sliced onion
1 tbsp. chopped garlic
1 pound spinach
¼ cup water
6 egg whites
4 full eggs
½ tsp. turmeric
½ tsp. kosher salt
½ tsp. black pepper

Directions:
Begin by preheating your oven to 350 degrees Fahrenheit. To the side, sauté your mushrooms in a large, oven-proof skillet. When they begin to brown, add onion and cook for an additional three minutes. Next, add the garlic and cook for just thirty seconds. Lastly, toss in your spinach and water. Cover the skillet and cook for two minutes. Your spinach should wilt. Next, remove the cover and cook until the entirety of the water has evaporated.

To the side, puree your egg whites, your full eggs, your turmeric, your salt, and your pepper in a blender. When your above skillet mixture no longer has water in it, pour the egg mixture over top.

Next, place your oven-proof skillet in the oven and bake for thirty minutes. The eggs should be set in the center. Serve at any temperature for a vibrant, nutrient-rich breakfast.

Gluten-Free Strawberry Crepes

Ingredients:
6 cups chopped strawberries
2 tbsp. honey

4 eggs
1 cup almond milk
2 tbsp. olive oil
1 tsp. vanilla extract
1 tbsp. light brown sugar
1/8 tsp. salt
¾ cup gluten-free flour

Directions:

In a medium-sized bowl, toss your strawberries, your honey, and your light brown sugar together. Allow them to assimilate together at room temperature for approximately thirty minutes.

Afterwards, whisk together the eggs, almond milk, and vanilla. Stir until combined. Next, add the gluten-free flour and the salt. The mixture should be completely combined.

Heat a non-stick skillet over medium-low. Add batter lightly to the bottom of the pan and swirl. When it begins to brown after about 45 seconds, flip the crepe. Cook an additional ten seconds. Repeat for the rest of the batter.

After the crepes have been fully cooked, place your strawberries in the crepe and serve. Enjoy the anti-inflammatory vitamin C feast before you.

Broccoli Avocado Salad

Ingredients:
1 lb. broccoli
1 avocado
2 tbsp. olive oil
2 tbsp. squeezed lemon juice
1 tbsp. grainy mustard

Directions:
Begin by trimming and slicing the broccoli into small pieces. Steam the broccoli until it's a bit crunchy. Drain and cool.

Next, peel the avocado and slice and dice it into small pieces. Place the avocado in a bowl with the broccoli.

To the side, whisk together the olive oil, squeezed lemon juice, and the grainy mustard in a small bowl.

Toss the broccoli and avocado salad together with the prepared dressing and enjoy this phytonutrient-rich, unsaturated fat feast.

Curry Cauliflower Soup

Ingredients:
1/3 cup cashews
2 tsp. olive oil
1 diced onion
1 chopped cauliflower
1 can coconut milk
2 tbsp. curry powder
1 tsp. turmeric
1 tsp. honey
¼ tsp. cinnamon
salt
¼ cup cilantro

Directions:
Begin by grounding the cashews in a blender or a food processor. Next, pour ¾ cup of water into the blender and blend for an additional two minutes. Next, mesh the cashew mixture through a strainer. Place the cashew mixture to the side.

Next, heat olive oil in a large pot on low. Toss in your diced onions and sauté for three minutes. Next, add the cauliflower, coconut milk, the prepared cashew milk, curry powder, turmeric, cumin, honey, cinnamon, and salt. Add water until it covers the entire mixture.

Continue to allow the soup to heat on low. The soup should simmer for about ten minutes.

Next, blend the soup in a blender. Look for your personal consistency. Garnish the soup with cilantro and serve hot. Enjoy your vitamin K-rich soup!

Anti-Inflammatory Quinoa Tabbouleh

Ingredients:
1 pound beets
2 cups quinoa
½ cup olive oil
¼ cup squeezed lemon juice
3 mashed garlic cloves
½ tsp. salt
1/3 cup chopped parsley
¼ cup chopped mint
3 chopped scallions
2 oz. arugula
½ pomegranate worth of seeds
¼ cup chopped almonds

Directions:
Begin by preheating the oven to 350 degrees Fahrenheit. Prepare a baking sheet by placing an aluminum foil lining over top. Pierce the beets several times with a fork and place the beets on the aluminum foil. Bake the beets for forty-five minutes. They should be tender.

Next, allow the beets to cool and peel the skin off of them. Remember to utilize paper towel or gloves; beets easily bleed onto the skin. Next, cut the beets into cubes and set aside.

To the side, bring four cups of water to a boil. Pour in the quinoa and lower the heat. Cover the pot and allow the quinoa to simmer for twenty minutes. Allow the quinoa to cool after it becomes fluffy.

Next, pour oil, lemon juice, salt, and garlic into a large serving bowl. Toss in the beets, quinoa, parsley, mint, scallions, and the arugula. Allow the salad dressing to assimilate over the rest of the tabbouleh. Serve with pomegranate seeds as garnish. Enjoy!

Pacific Tofu Lunch Recipe

Ingredients:
12 oz. organic tofu cut into slices
6 tbsp. low sodium organic soy sauce
2 green onions
1 garlic clove
1 tsp. cornstarch
¾ tsp. agar powder
¾ cup hot water
¼ cup agave syrup
1 ½ tsp. vegetarian broth
½ tsp. powdered ginger
½ tsp. ground mustard powder
14 oz. pineapple chunks
1 seeded and sliced red pepper

Directions:
Begin by preheating the oven to 500 degrees Fahrenheit. On the stovetop, brown up the tofu slices in a pan. Next, spread the tofu out in a baking pan in a single layer.

Pour the soy sauce, onion, garlic, cornstarch, and agar powder into a blender. Blend for approximately two minutes. Next, add the hot water, agave syrup, vegetarian broth, ginger, and mustard powder. Continue to blend until the mixture is smooth. Afterwards, place the mixture in a saucepan and allow it to come to a boil.

Place the prepared pineapple and the pepper into the pre-boiled mixture. Next, pour the mixture over the tofu. Allow the tofu to bake for fifteen minutes.

Serve this cardiovascular-boosting tofu hot or cold. Enjoy!

Autumn Squash and Apple Soup

Ingredients:
1 large peeled and chopped butternut squash
2 quartered onions
3 garlic cloves
2 peeled and quartered apples
2 tbsp. olive oil
salt and chili powder to taste
4-5 cups vegetable stock

Directions:
Begin by preheating the oven to 400 degrees Fahrenheit.
Prepare a roasting pan with pre-cut squash, onions, garlic, and apples. Coat them well with oil. Shake salt and chili powder overtop. Roast the vegetables and fruit in the oven for forty minutes. Be certain to check on them and stir every ten minutes.
Next, place half of your roasted vegetables into a food processor along with two cups of vegetable stock. Purée the mixture until it's smooth. Repeat with the remaining broth and vegetables. If the soup is too thick, you can always add more broth.
Afterwards, bring the soup to a slight simmer prior to serving. Enjoy this carotene, vitamin-rich lunch dish.

Fennel Strawberry Salad

Ingredients:
4 cups baby arugula
1 cup sliced fennel
12 sliced strawberries
2 tbsp. chopped mint
6 tbsp. balsamic vinaigrette
¼ cup sliced almonds

Directions:
Place the baby arugula, sliced fennel, sliced strawberries, and the chopped mint together in a salad bowl. Toss the salad and allow the ingredients to mix. Next, pour on the balsamic vinaigrette and serve with sliced almonds overtop.
Enjoy this different take on the springtime salad. Feast in the anti-cancer strawberry components and the phytonutrient-packed fennel.

Vegetable-Rich Lentil Soup

Ingredients:
1 lb. lentils
1 bay leaf
3 sliced carrots
2 chopped celery stalks
1 chopped onion
½ tsp. cumin
2 cups crushed tomatoes
2 tbsp. olive oil
salt and pepper to taste

Directions:

Place the lentils in a large pot with water covering it by six inches. Add the bay leaf to the water, as well. Bring the pot to boil and then lower the heat. Allow the lentils to simmer for 30 minutes until they're tender.

Toss carrots, celery, cumin, and the onion into the lentils. Cook an additional thirty minutes.

Next, add the tomatoes, olive oil, and salt and pepper. Simmer until the lentils are creamy. Serve the soup warm as a healthy dose of fiber and antioxidants ready to boost you through your day.

Papaya Salsa and Lemon Baked Halibut

Papaya Salsa Ingredients:
½ cup cilantro
1 cup diced papaya
¼ cup diced red bell pepper
¼ cup diced onion
1 minced jalapeno pepper
2 tbsp. squeezed lime juice

Marinade Ingredients:
3 tbsp. squeezed lemon juice
1 tbsp. grated lemon zest
1 tbsp. olive oil
1 tbsp. grated ginger
¾ tsp. black pepper
½ cup cilantro

Further Ingredients:
Six 6 oz. halibut steaks
3 sliced fennel bulbs
2/3 cup water
9 black peppercorns

Directions:
Begin by preparing the salsa. Place the minced cilantro, diced papaya, peppers, onion, jalapeno, and the squeezed lemon juice in a small bowl. Mix and cover. Store in the refrigerator.

Next, prepare the marinade. In a medium-sized bowl, pour the lemon juice, lemon zest, oil, ginger, pepper, and cilantro. Allow this mixture to assimilate together for about two hours. After the two hours, place the halibut steaks in a baking pan. Pour the marinade over top of the steaks and cover the steaks. Allow the steaks to marinate in the refrigerator for about a half hour.

Preheat the oven to 400 degrees Fahrenheit. To the side, cook the sliced fennel bulbs in 2/3 cup of water over high heat. Cook for just eight minutes. Next, remove the halibut from the refrigerator and bake them in the preheated oven for just five minutes. Flip, and bake for an additional five minutes. Place a layer of fennel on each serving plate and place the halibut piece on top of the fennel. Drizzle the papaya salsa on top. Enjoy your protein and vitamin-rich entrée!

Vegetarian's Delight Shepherd's Pie

Ingredients:
2 peeled and cubed sweet potatoes
6 peeled and cubed white potatoes
1 tbsp. olive oil
1 tbsp. Italian seasoning
1 tbsp. Cajun seasoning

Filling Ingredients:
3 ¼ cups water
1 bay leaf
1 cup lentils
2 tsp. Cajun seasoning
1 cup sliced onions
2 cloves garlic

1 cup sliced shiitake mushrooms
½ cup broccoli
½ cup red bell pepper
1 tbsp. olive oil
1 tsp. curry powder
1 tsp. salt
1 tbsp. cornstarch
1 sliced zucchini

Directions:
Begin by preheating the oven to 350 degrees Fahrenheit.
To the side, bring water to boil in a large pot. Plop the chopped sweet potatoes and white potatoes into the boiling water. Allow them to simmer for forty-five minutes. Next, strain the potatoes. Keep two cups of the strained water, and pour one of these cups back into the pot with the potatoes. Mash the potatoes in the water. Next, add olive oil, Italian seasoning, and 1 tsp. of the Cajun seasoning. Continue to mash.
Bring three additional cups of water to a boil on the stovetop. Toss in the bay leaf, the lentils, and the rest of the Cajun seasoning. Cook for forty-five minutes.
Fry the onions, garlic, mushrooms, broccoli, and the bell peppers in olive oil in a saucepan for about four minutes. Next, pour the additional reserved cup of water from the potato boil to this vegetable mixture. Toss in the salt and curry powder as well. Pour the entire mixture into the pot with the pre-cooked lentils.
Dissolve cornstarch in ¼ cup water.

Soy Tempeh Spicy Stir-Fry

Ingredients:
1 ½ lbs. sliced soy tempeh

Marinade Ingredients:

3 tbsp. low sodium organic soy sauce
1 ½ tbsp. rice wine
1 ½ tbsp. minced shallots
1 tsp. avocado oil
2 tbsp. olive oil

Seasoning Ingredients:
2 tbsp. chopped red chili
2 tbsp. chopped garlic
2 sliced onions
1 ½ cup shredded basil leaves

Sauce Ingredients:
2 tbsp. fish sauce
1 ½ tbsp. low sodium organic soy sauce
1 tbsp. honey
1 ½ tbsp. water

Directions:
Begin by preparing the marinade in a small bowl: add the soy sauce, rice wine, minced shallots, avocado, and olive oil. Place the tempeh in a large bowl and pour the marinade over top of it. Allow the tempeh to marinate for twenty minutes.

Next, heat a skillet with 1 tbsp. olive oil on high in order to sear the tempeh. Place the tempeh on the hot skillet for three minutes on each side. Allow the tempeh to cool immediately after.

Next, utilize the same skillet. Toss in the seasoning ingredients: red chilies, chopped garlic, onions, and the shredded basil leaves. Stir-fry until the onions begin to brown. While the onions brown, prepare the sauce to the side in a small bowl: mix together the fish sauce, soy sauce, honey, and water. Stir. Then add the sauce to the stir-fry. Bring the mixture in the skillet to a boil.

Place the seared tempeh in the boiling sauce and baste. Serve the tempeh immediately after to enjoy all the benefits of this cancer-fighting, anti-inflammatory dinner.

Pistachio-Crusted Chicken

Ingredients:
2 boneless chicken cutlets
¼ cup rice flour
1 beaten egg
¼ cup water
¼ cup finely chopped pistachios
1 tbsp. olive oil

Directions:
Begin by preheating the oven to 350 degrees Fahrenheit.

Prepare the chicken cutlets. Salt them lightly and coat them with rice flour. Crack open the egg into a bowl and add ¼ cup water. Furthermore, add the chopped pistachios to a separate bowl. Coat each floured cutlet with the egg mixture. Next, cover each cutlet with pistachios.

Place the pistachio-coated culets in a skillet with a tbsp. of olive oil. Heat the chicken and sauté each side for approximately five minutes. Next, reposition the skillet into the preheated oven and bake the chicken for an additional fifteen minutes. Serve with your choice of vegetables for a balanced, protein-rich meal.

Spicy Tomato Gazpacho

Ingredients:
5 lbs. chopped heirloom tomatoes
1 can diced tomatoes
2 diced celery stalks
1 chopped chili
1 diced bell pepper
1 diced onion
½ cup diced jicama
1 diced cucumber
¼ cup chopped Italian parsley
1 tbsp. chopped cilantro
1/3 cup red wine vinegar
2 tbsp. olive oil
2 tsp. vegetarian Worcestershire sauce
1 ½ tsp. green Tabasco sauce
2 tsp. salt
2 tsp. coriander
1 tsp. cumin
½ tsp. cayenne

Directions:
Place all the listed ingredients into a large bowl with ¼ cup chilled water. Mix the ingredients to combine well. Place three cups of this mixture into a blender and blend until smooth. Return the blended mixture to the greater mixture and stir. Cover the gazpacho and chill in the refrigerator. Serve the dish cold.

Smoked Salmon Seaweed Rolls

Ingredients:
8 sheets nori (seaweed)
8 pieces wild smoked salmon
1 sliced cucumber
1 sliced red bell pepper
2 sliced avocados
24 mint leaves
24 cilantro leaves
Wasabi Ingredients:
1 cup shelled edamame
¼ cup water
3 tbsp. olive oil
2 tbsp. lime juice
1 tbsp. fresh cilantro
2 tsp. wasabi powder
½ tsp. salt

Directions:
Begin by preparing the wasabi by placing all the listed ingredients in a food processor and blending it until its smooth. Taste and add more lime juice if necessary.
Place sheets of nori on a clean workspace. Spread two tablespoons of the wasabi mixture onto each sheet of nori.
Next, place 1 piece of salmon, 2 cucumber slices, 2 bell pepper slices, and 2 avocado slices in the nori on top of the wasabi mix.

Top each nori slice with 3 mint leaves and 3 cilantro leaves. Roll up the nori rolls into proper sushi rolls. Afterwards, cut each nori roll into eight pieces and enjoy the protein-rich, antioxidant-stocked salmon roll!

Ginger Snap Cookies

Ingredients:
2/3 cup molasses
1/3 cup butter substitute (Spectrum Spread works well)
¼ cup apple juice
1 tsp. vanilla
2 egg whites
4 cups rice flour
½ cup stevia
2 tsp. powdered ginger
1 tsp. cinnamon
1/3 tsp. powdered cloves
¼ tsp. allspice
½ tsp. salt
1 tsp. baking soda
½ tsp. baking powder
1/8 tsp. grated orange zest

Directions:
Begin by preheating the oven to 350 degrees Fahrenheit.
To the side in a large bowl, pour the molasses, butter substitute, apple juice, and the vanilla into a large bowl. Mix well.
In a separate bowl, add your egg whites and beat them for three minutes. Pour the egg white mixture into the molasses mixture. Whisk well.
In a separate, large bowl, mix the dry ingredients: orange zest, rice flour, stevia, powdered ginger, cinnamon, powdered cloves, allspice, salt, baking soda, and baking powder.

Add the dry ingredients to the wet ingredients and stir well. The dough should be stiff, firm.

Roll the dough out with a rolling pin and cut out cookies with a cookie-cutter. Place the cookies on a prepared, oiled cooking sheet and bake for about twelve minutes. The cookies should be golden brown. Allow them to cool prior to enjoying this anti-inflammatory dessert.

Blueberry Peach Mid-Afternoon Cobbler

Filling Ingredients:
5 peeled and sliced peaches
1 cup blueberries
¼ cup orange juice
½ cup stevia
pinch of nutmeg
2 tsp. cornstarch

Biscuit Ingredients:
5 tbsp. butter substitute (Spectrum Spread works well)
2 cups rice flour
1 tbsp. stevia
1 tbsp. baking powder
½ tsp. salt
¾ cup almond milk

Directions:
Begin by preheating the oven to 400 degrees Fahrenheit.

Next, add the filling ingredients: sliced peaches, blueberries, orange juice, stevia, nutmeg, and cornstarch to a saucepan. Bring the ingredients to a boil and then turn down the heat. Allow it to simmer until it thickens. Place the filling in a saucepan and spread evenly on the bottom.

To the side, mix together the butter substitute, rice flour, stevia, salt, and almond milk. Remember to mix slowly. Knead the dough on a floured surface. Utilize a cookie cutter to form ten biscuits. Place the biscuits overtop the fruit filling. Bake the cobbler in the oven for twenty minutes. Allow them to cool for ten minutes prior to serving. Enjoy this anti-oxidant rich, fortifying dessert.

Almond Pineapple Coconut Milkshake

Ingredients:
¼ cup almonds
1 cup chopped pineapple
½ cup crushed ice
½ tsp. maple syrup
¼ cup coconut milk
½ cup pineapple juice

Directions:
Place the ½ cup almonds in the blender for an initial blend. Next, add the rest of the ingredients. Blend everything until the milkshake is smooth. Enjoy the monounsaturated fat and the vitamin E supplied by the almonds.

Choco-Banana Frozen Potassium-Rich Dessert

Ingredients:
4 bananas
2 tbsp. unsweetened cocoa powder
1 tsp. vanilla
2 tbsp. maple syrup

Directions:
Peel the bananas and place them in a food processor with the cocoa powder. Next, add the vanilla and the maple syrup. Blend the

mixture until it smooth. Next, place the mixture into small, individual cups. Freeze the mixture until it's just frozen prior to serving. Enjoy this magnesium and potassium-rich dessert on a hot summer day.

Walnut and Eggplant Pâté

Ingredients:
1 eggplant
1 cup walnut pieces
2 tsp. peeled and chopped ginger root
2 cloves mashed garlic
1 tbsp. olive oil
1/8 tsp. ground allspice
salt and pepper to taste
Directions:
Begin by preheating the oven to 450 degrees Fahrenheit. Push a fork through the eggplant in various places and place the eggplant in the oven for forty-five minutes.

While you allow the eggplant to bake, place the walnuts in a food processor and grind until the walnuts are fine.

Remove the eggplant from the oven. It should be soft. Allow the steam to escape and then scrape the pulp into the food processor. Add the ginger root, the garlic, and the olive oil. Process the mixture until it is smooth.

Add the pre-ground walnuts and allspice to the mixture as well. Continue to process. When it is finished, season it with salt and pepper and allow it to chill in the refrigerator. It should be firm upon serving.

Green Power-Hour Drink

Ingredients:
1 ½ cups almond milk
1 banana

3 large kale leaves
5 pitted dates
1 tbsp. hemp protein powder

Directions:
Add the almond milk, banana, kale leaves, pitted dates, and the protein powder to a high-speed blender. Blend the mixture until the drink is smooth. This snack lends a boost at any hour of any day.

Best Brussels Sprouts

Ingredients:
1 lb. Brussels sprouts
2 tbsp. olive oil
1 diced onion
1 tsp. red pepper flakes
¼ tsp. nutmeg
salt to taste

Directions:
Slice and dice the pound of Brussels sprouts. Heat olive oil in a skillet on medium heat and toss in your sliced onions, red pepper flakes, and salt. Sauté and stir. The onion should begin to brown.
Next, toss in the sprouts. Continue to sauté until the sprouts become a bright green approximately five minutes later. Add the nutmeg. Turn off the heat, and serve hot. This is the true, proper way to eat these nutrient-rich, cancer-fighting vegetables!

Mediterranean Recipes

Mediterranean Scrambled Eggs

Ingredients:
4 eggs
1 yellow-pepper, diced
2 sliced spring onions
8 quartered cherry tomatoes
2 tablespoon of sliced olives
1 tablespoon of capers
1 tablespoon of olive oil
¼ teaspoon of dried oregano
Black pepper
Fresh parsley

Preparation:
Start by heating one tablespoon of olive oil in a skillet and adding the diced yellow pepper and sliced onions. Stew these for a few minutes, only to then add tomatoes, capers, and olives. Continue to cooking on a medium heat for one minute.
Once the vegetables are ready, crack your eggs and scramble them into the veg. Cook for a few minutes, stirring the eggs constantly, to achieve the velvety texture. While you are doing that, add the black pepper and oregano, and should you want to, a pinch of salt.
Now that your scrambled eggs with veggies are ready, serve them on a plate and top it off with some fresh chopped parsley.

Watermelon Pizza with Feta and Balsamic

Ingredients:
1 watermelon slice
1 oz./28 g Feta cheese
6 olives (Kalamata)

1 tsp fresh mint leaves

½ tablespoons balsamic sauce

Preparation:

You should start by slicing a watermelon in half. From one half, take a 1" thick slice and lay it flat. Slice this piece into "pizza triangles" and this will be your pizza base.

You will need a round pan/plate that is usually used for baking pizza, on which you will put the watermelon wedges (pizza slices), arranging them in a circular fashion. Start by covering those wedges in feta cheese, and add olives next. Top it all off with balsamic sauce and fresh mint leaves. Voila, you are set and good to go as this recipe requires no baking or grilling!

Pizza with Avocado, Tomato, and Gouda Cheese

Ingredients:
For Crust
1 cup chickpea flour
1 cup cold water
2 tablespoons olive oil
¼ teaspoons sea salt
¼ teaspoon black pepper
1 teaspoon minced garlic
1 teaspoon onion powder

For Toppings
1 sliced Roma tomato
Half of an avocado
2 oz./28 g thinly sliced Gouda cheese
⅓ cup tomato sauce
3 tablespoons green onions
Extra pepper, red flakes to top

Preparation:
Mix all the ingredients for the crust, until you get a batter like texture. Whisk either using a fork or using a hand mixer until the batter is smooth. Once that is done, let the batter sit for around 20 minutes at regular room temperature. While you are waiting for it to rest, preheat the pan in an oven at 425 degrees F/220 degrees Celsius (10 minutes).

Prepare your vegetables needed for the topping. Carefully take out the pan out the oven, and put it aside. Coat the pan in olive oil and then pour in the chickpea batter. Tilt the pan as much as you need until it is completely covered in the batter. Once that is set, put the pan back in the oven for another 8 minutes at the same temperature.

Take the crust out the oven and add the tomato sauce and vegetables. Ensure you spread the tomato sauce over the baked crust, and continue by putting tomatoes and avocado on top. After that, you should sprinkle thinly sliced Gouda cheese, green onions and a little drizzle of olive oil. Continue baking for about 15 minutes or until the crust is brown and crispy.

Take the pan out of the oven. Allow to cool for 5 minutes. Sprinkle some more pepper and red flakes on top and serve.

Keto Egg Muffins with Prosciutto

Ingredients:
9 Slices Prosciutto
½ cup of canned roasted red pepper, sliced + additional for garnish
⅓ cup of fresh spinach, minced
¼ cup of feta cheese, crumbled
5 large eggs
A pinch of salt
A pinch of pepper
1 ½ tablespoons of Pesto sauce
Some fresh basil for garnish

Preparation:
Preheat your oven to 400°F/200°C, and coating the muffin tin using a non-stick cooking spray. Cover the base of each muffin spot with one and a half slice of Prosciutto, and continue by placing roasted red pepper over it (not too much). Once you have done that it is time to top it all off with ½ tablespoon of feta cheese.

In a medium bowl, whisk the eggs together with the salt and pepper. Make sure that the mixture is smooth and easily divided. Pour the same amount in each muffin tin.

Bake for 15 minutes, or until you can see that the eggs are set. Once it is baked, remove the muffin and use the parsley and a bit more roasted red paper for garnishing.

Greek Guacamole

Ingredients:
2 large ripe avocados (halved, pit removed)
2 tablespoons of lemon juice
1 heaped tablespoon of chopped sun-dried tomatoes
3 tablespoons of diced cherry tomatoes
¼ cup of diced red onion
1 teaspoons of dried oregano
2 tablespoons of fresh chopped parsley
4 whole kalamata olives (pitted and chopped)
1 pinch each of sea salt and black pepper

Preparation:
In a medium bowl, add the avocado and lemon juice together, using a potato masher or a fork. Once you have done that, it is time to add remaining the ingredients including tomatoes and olives. Add spices to suit your preference.

For added acidity, add some more lemon juice, or alternatively, for some kick, add some parsley or oregano. For a deeper flavor, leave it in the fridge overnight. Add some parsley for garnish, just before serving.

Feta Inspired Frozen Yo

Ingredients:
1 cup of plain Greek yogurt
½ cup of feta cheese
1 tablespoons honey

Preparation:
Put all the ingredients in a wide bowl and mix until it all combines. Pour it in a food processor and let it run until you achieve a smooth texture. After that, return it to the wide bowl, and put it in a freezer. Freeze until the mixture becomes solid.

Break it into cubes and return it to blender. Try to achieve a creamy, yogurt-like consistency. You can add some water or milk to aid you in the process. Serve immediately with a drizzle of honey on top.

Sweet Potatoes Stuffed with Avocado-Tahini and Chickpeas

Ingredients:
8 medium-sized potatoes
Marinated Chickpeas
15oz./420 g can of chickpeas, drained and rinsed
½ a red pepper, diced
3 tablespoons of extra virgin olive oil
1 tablespoon of fresh lemon juice
1 tablespoon of lemon zest
1 clove of garlic, crushed
1 tablespoon of freshly chopped parsley
1 tablespoon of fresh oregano
¼ teaspoon of sea salt
Avocado-Tahini Sauce
1 medium-sized ripe avocado
¼ cup of tahini
¼ cup water
1 clove of garlic, crushed
1 tablespoon of fresh parsley
1 tablespoon of fresh lemon juice

Toppings:
¼ cup of pepitas

Crumbled up vegan feta (for the dairy free version)
Preparation:
Preheat the oven to 400°F/200°C. Place all the potatoes on a baking tray and pierce a few holes through each, in order to prevent the air from staying trapped.
Bake for about an hour until the potatoes are tender and brown.
Combine the chickpeas with the ingredients for the marinade and let it sit for 45 minutes.
For the avocado-tahini sauce, add all the ingredients to a blender and process until you achieve a smooth consistency. If it seems too thick, simply add more water.
Once the potatoes are out, let them cool down for 10 minutes. Then slit the potatoes down the middle and spoon the marinated chickpeas in. Top it all off with the avocado-tahini sauce, and serve immediately.

Refreshing Tuna Salad

Ingredients:
10oz./280 g of drained Tuna
2 tablespoons of capers
8 sliced of Kalamata olives
¼ cup of diced red peppers
1 tablespoons of lemon juice
2tablespoons of olive oil
Salt and pepper to taste

Preparation:
Combine all the ingredients in a medium bowl, and whisk with a fork, until all is well combined.
You can serve it over a muffin or lettuce immediately, or after a few hours left in the fridge

Greek Plate of Steak and Hummus

Ingredients:
1 lb/1 kg of beef (Top Sirloin Steaks Boneless, cut 1 inch thick)
1 medium cucumber
3 tablespoons of fresh lemon juice
¼ teaspoon of pepper
1 cup of ready-to-serve hummus
Romesco sauce
Rub:
¼ cup oregano leaves (chopped)
1 tablespoon of grated lemon peel
1 tablespoon of garlic
1 teaspoon of pepper

Preparation:
Start by mixing the rub ingredients together and pressing them into the sliced beef tenderloin.
Place your steaks on a grill, letting them sit there from 10 to 17 minutes depending on how you like your beef done (turn occasionally).
Slice and prepare the cucumber by mixing it with the lemon juice and pepper.
Once the steaks are done, carve them into slices and sprinkle some salt and pepper to taste.
Serve with ¼ cup of hummus on each side, and Romesco sauce drizzled on top of the beef.
 Garnish with sliced cucumber, pita chips, or olives.

Beef and Veggie Wraps

Ingredients:
12 oz./ 336 g sliced cooked beef (steak)
4 whole wheat flour tortillas

Hummus
Peppers, carrots, tomatoes (to taste)
Spinach, arugula (to taste)
Preparation:
Cover a skillet with a non-stick cooking spray. Heat the whole wheat tortillas over medium temperature for about one minute on each side.
Spread hummus evenly leaving about ¼ inch uncovered around the edges.
Mix the vegetables and greens and add on top of the hummus.
Top it all off with sliced beef and roll firmly.

Steak Pinwheels

Ingredients:
1 lb./ 450 g beef steak
⅓ cup of lemon juice
2 tablespoons of olive oil
2 tablespoons of dried oregano leaves
⅓ cup of olive tapenade
¼ cup of crumbled feta cheese
1 cup of frozen spinach
4 cups of cherry tomatoes
Salt to taste

Preparation:
Cover the beef in plastic wrap and pound it up to around ½ inches of thickness. Remove from plastic.
Mix olive oil, dried oregano leaves and lemon juice as marinade ingredients, and coat both sides of the flank. Leave it in a bag to refrigerate for around 4 hours.
Preheat the oven to 425°F/220°C
Placing baking paper over a baking sheet.

Take out your steak and place it on a cutting board. Spread the tapenade and top it off with spinach and feta.

Roll the steak into a log and tie it up using kitchen strings. Slice it into six even pieces, and pour the remains of the marinade over it. Arrange tomatoes around the beef pinwheels.

Roast for around 30 minutes or until tender

Allow to cool for 5 minutes.

Mediterranean Salad Burger

Ingredients:
4 cooked Ground beef burgers (3 oz./75 g)
2 cups of chopped cucumber
2 cups of Romaine lettuce
2 cups of chopped tomatoes
½ cup of diced red onion
½ cup of reduced fat Greek-dressing
¼ cup of crumbled feta cheese
2 tablespoons of Kalamata olives

Preparation:
Microwave the burgers for about 2 minutes.
Combine the vegetables in a medium bowl, and toss them around with the Greek dressing.
Divide the vegetable mixture onto four plates.
Place the burger on top of the lettuce mixture and top it off with some Kalamata olives and crumbled Feta cheese. Serve immediately.

Mediterranean Kofta Beef

Ingredients:
1 pound/453 g Ground Beef (93% lean or leaner)
½ cup of diced onions

1 tablespoon of olive oil
½ teaspoon of salt
½ teaspoon of ground coriander
½ teaspoon of ground cumin
¼ teaspoon of ground cinnamon
¼ teaspoon of all-spice
¼ teaspoon of dried mint leaves
Preparation:

In a large bowl, combine the beef, onion, salt, coriander, cumin, cinnamon, all-spice and mint leaves. Mix gently, but thoroughly.

Taking a quarter of the beef mixture, shape is around 8" skewers. Be sure to leave about 1" or 2" at the bottom of the skewer.

With your fingers, make small dents along the beef kofta, about 1" apart.

Continue this process with the rest of the kofta mixture and 3 skewers.

Chill in the fridge for a minimum of 10 minutes.

Grill the koftas in the center of a warm grill. Try to avoid turning them too soon, as they could break. Grill for 12 – 14 minutes, or until cooked through.

Mediterranean Lemony Chicken Soup

Ingredients:
1 tablespoon of olive oil
3/4 cup of carrot, cubed
½ cup of chopped yellow onion
2 teaspoons minced fresh garlic
¾ teaspoon of crushed red pepper
6 cups unsalted chicken stock
½ cup of uncooked whole-wheat orzo
3 large eggs
¼ cup of fresh lemon juice
3 cups of shredded rotisserie chicken
3 cups of chopped baby spinach
1¼ teaspoons of kosher salt
½ teaspoon of black pepper
3 tablespoons of chopped fresh dill

Preparation:

Prepare a Dutch oven by lightly coating it with extra virgin olive oil. Heat it to a medium temperature and start cooking onions and carrots together for about 3 to 4 minutes. Once carrots and onions have softened, add garlic and red pepper. Continue stirring for a couple of minutes.

Add stock to the pot and bring everything to boiling. Add whole wheat orzo and cook it together until it is al dente.

Whisk the eggs and the lemon juice together in a medium bowl, gradually adding stock while you are mixing.

Lower the heat to low and mix in egg-lemon juice mixture, chicken, spinach, salt and the pepper into the pot. Cook for a few minutes more or until spinach wilts.

Divide the soup into six separate bowls and sprinkle some fresh dill on top.

Quick Chicken Marsala

Ingredients:

2 tablespoons of olive oil, divided between 2 separate tablespoons

4 skinless, boneless chicken breast cutlets

¾ teaspoon of black pepper, divided into ¼ and ½ teaspoons

½ teaspoon of kosher salt, divided into ¼'s

10 oz./280 g. pre-sliced button mushrooms

4 thyme sprigs

1 tablespoon of all-purpose flour

2/3 cup of unsalted chicken stock

2/3 cup of Marsala wine

2 ½ tablespoons of unsalted butter

1 tablespoon of chopped fresh thyme

Preparation:

Heat one of your tablespoons of olive oil in a non-stick pan.

Season your chicken breast cutlets with the ¼ teaspoon of salt and ½ teaspoon of pepper.

Cook for 4 minutes per side, until the chicken is golden brown.

Once the chicken is done remove it from the pan without wiping the oils and the juice that chicken has released.

To the same pan, add another tablespoon of olive oil, mushrooms, and thyme sprigs. Cook for around 6 minutes until browned.

Add flour and continue stirring for a minute more.

Add the wine and stock to the pan, bringing everything to boiling.

Add the remaining spices, and bring the chicken back to the pan. Cook for a few more minutes, and remove the sprigs just before the end. Serve with pita as a side.

Lamb and Beet Meatballs

Ingredients:

10 oz./280 g vacuum-packed cooked beets (such as Love Beets)

½ cup of uncooked bulgur

1 teaspoon of ground cumin

¾ teaspoon of kosher salt, divided into ½ and ¼ teaspoons

¾ teaspoon of freshly ground black pepper

6oz./168 g of ground lamb

⅓ cup of almond flour

1 tablespoon of olive oil

½ cup of grated cucumber

½ cup of reduced-fat sour-cream

2 tablespoons of thinly sliced fresh mint

2 tablespoons of fresh lemon juice

4 cups mixed baby greens

Preparation:

Start by preheating the oven to 425°F/204°C.

In a blender, process the beets until they are finely chopped.

Combine the lamb meat, beets, cumin, bulgur, salt, pepper and almond flour in a large bowl. Go for 12 smaller meatballs.

Once meatballs have been shaped, cook them in a non-stick skillet for about 4 minutes or until you see a nice brown coating.

Place the whole pan, with the meatballs, in the preheated oven and bake for around 8 minutes.

In another mixing bowl, combine cucumber, sour cream, lemon juice, sea salt and mint to make a light dressing.

Take the pan out of the oven and serve the meatballs on four plates. Top it all off with the dressing and use greens for side garnishing.

Zucchini-Sausage Pizza with Pesto Sauce

Ingredients:
3 oz./75 g ground mild Italian turkey sausage
1 cup thinly sliced zucchini
4 tablespoons of refrigerated basil pesto, divided into 1 and 3 tablespoons
1 pkg. of 3 (7-inch) prebaked pizza crusts (such as Mama Marys)
3 oz./75 g fresh, thinly sliced mozzarella cheese
⅛ teaspoon of crushed red pepper
2 tablespoons of fresh basil leaves

Preparation:
Heat a non-stick skillet on a medium-high temperature and add the ground sausage to it. Cook for around 5 minutes, breaking the sausage in the process using a spoon or a fork. Once it is cooked, remove it from the pan, without wiping the oil or juice.

Add the zucchini and a tablespoon of pesto sauce to the same pan, cooking for about 3 minutes.

Preheat your oven to 450°F/220°C.

Place the pizza crusts on a baking sheet and use the remaining pesto sauce (3 tablespoons) to cover the base.

Top the crust with the zucchini mixture, sausages, red pepper, and some crumbled mozzarella.

Bake for around 6-8 minutes and remove from the oven. Add a finishing touch by sprinkling some basil leaves and a little bit more of mozzarella.

Anti-anging Recipes

Roasted Garlic Served on Crostini

There are countless variations of this classic recipe. The garlic and olive oil will keep inflammation at bay and tantalize your taste buds. You can also try adding herbs such as thyme, sage, or rosemary to "wow" your guests.

Ingredients
1 bulb garlic
2 tablespoons virgin olive oil
½ bunch fresh parsley
½ loaf baguette

Directions
Preheat oven to 375°F.
Cut off the top quarter of the garlic bulb. Rub both cut sides of garlic with olive oil, then place the top back on the bulb and wrap in foil. Place in the oven and bake until the cloves are fork tender, about 5 to 10 minutes.
While the garlic cooks, chop the parsley. Slice the baguette thinly on the bias. Brush with the oil and place on a baking sheet. Toast until light brown.
Serve the bulb intact on a platter surrounded by crostini and sprinkled with parsley.

Marinated Portobello Mushrooms

Portobello mushrooms have such a meaty flavor that they can be used in place of meat in many recipes. They will boost your fiber, protein, and B vitamin intake. They also give you a nice dose of the antioxidants vitamin C and selenium. Free radicals beware!

Ingredients

6 portobello mushrooms

1 teaspoon extra-virgin olive oil

2 teaspoons balsamic vinegar

Pinch of iodized salt

Freshly cracked black pepper, to taste

¼ bunch marjoram

¼ bunch oregano

Directions

Remove the stems from the caps of the mushrooms and scrape out the black membrane. Slice the stems in half.

Mix together the remaining ingredients. Combine the caps and stems with the marinade in a plastic container; marinate for at least 3 hours.

Preheat oven to 400°F.

Roast the mushrooms for 15 to 20 minutes on oven rack. Cut the caps into small wedges and serve.

Vegetable Kebabs

Talk about a serious phytochemical concoction. Inflammation will shy away from this appetizer. Serve these kebabs as an appetizer at parties so your guests can easily handle the food without using cutlery.

Ingredients

Wooden skewers

12 scallions

1 large red pepper

1 large yellow pepper
1 large green pepper
12 large button mushrooms
1 tablespoon olive oil
Freshly cracked black pepper, to taste
Kosher salt, to taste

Directions
Cut standard wooden skewers in half for appetizer-size portions, then soak the skewers in water for a minimum of 1 hour.
Preheat grill or broiler.
Trim off the roots and dark green parts of the scallions. Dice the peppers into large pieces.
Thread the vegetables on to the skewers, and brush all sides of the vegetables with oil. Season with pepper and salt.
Place the skewers on the grill or under the broiler, paying close attention as they cook, as they can easily burn. Cook until the vegetables are fork tender.

Soaking the Skewers
When using wooden skewers in cooking, always soak them in water for an hour before spearing the food items. Soaking the skewers allows you to place them on the grill for a time without them burning.

Haddock Fish Cakes

This version of a familiar fish cake has the fresh flavor of haddock. Serve this with a spicy sauce or a fresh spritz of lemon.

Ingredients
1 pound haddock
2 leeks
1 red pepper
2 egg whites

Pinch of kosher salt
Freshly cracked black pepper, to taste
1 tablespoon olive oil
Directions
Finely shred the raw fish with a fork. Dice the leeks and red pepper. Combine all the ingredients except the oil in a medium-size bowl; mix well. Form the mixture into small oval patties.

Heat the oil in a medium-size sauté pan. Place the cakes in the pan and loosely cover with the lid; sauté the cakes for 4 to 6 minutes on each side. Drain on a rack covered with paper towels; serve immediately.

Thai Peanut Sauce

This is a great sauce for grilled or broiled chicken and beef skewers. It will keep in the refrigerator, covered, for up to a week. Bring to room temperature before serving.

Ingredients
2 tablespoons water
¼ cup creamy peanut butter
2 tablespoons tamari
1 teaspoon red pepper flakes
2 teaspoons sesame oil
2 tablespoons chopped unsalted peanuts, for garnish (optional)

Directions
Place all the ingredients (except the peanuts) in the bowl of a food processor fitted with a metal blade or in a blender (or blend by hand with a sturdy whisk); cover and process until smooth. Add a little more water if necessary to adjust the consistency.
Place the sauce in a small serving bowl and garnish with the chopped peanuts.

Island-Style Shrimp Cocktail

A nice twist on the traditional shrimp cocktail. And it's easy to pack up to take to summer outdoor barbecues.

Ingredients
1 teaspoon minced garlic
¼ teaspoon salt
1 tablespoon minced fresh ginger
3 tablespoons finely chopped scallions
1 tablespoon finely chopped jalapeño pepper
¼ cup freshly squeezed lime juice
Sugar substitute equal to 2 tablespoons sugar
1 tablespoon canola oil
1 pound extra-large (21- to 25-count) shrimp, peeled, tails left on
¼ teaspoon salt
¼ teaspoon ground black pepper

Lemon and lime wedges

Directions
Combine the garlic, salt, ginger, scallions, jalapeño, lime juice, and sugar substitute in a small serving bowl and set aside.

Heat the oil in a medium-size, heavy-bottomed nonstick skillet over high heat until it starts to smoke. Season the shrimp with salt and pepper. Add the shrimp to the skillet and sauté until cooked through, about 2 minutes. Remove skillet from heat and immediately add 2 tablespoons of the jalapeño-lime sauce to the skillet; toss to coat the shrimp.

Transfer the shrimp to a baking sheet to cool for about 5 minutes. To serve, arrange the shrimp on a platter with the bowl of sauce. Garnish with lemon and lime wedges.

Turkey Meatballs with Fruit Sauce

This is a tasty change of pace. The fruit complements the turkey beautifully. Use ground turkey breast, which contains white meat only.

Ingredients
Olive oil
2 slices toasted 100% whole-wheat bread
1 pound ground turkey breast
¼ cup dried cranberries
¼ cup chopped pecans
1 egg
¼ teaspoon cinnamon
¼ teaspoon curry powder
Pinch of kosher salt
Freshly cracked black pepper, to taste
½ cup Apple Chutney

Directions

Preheat oven to 350°F. Brush a baking dish with oil.

Soak the bread in water until completely saturated and then squeeze out the excess liquid. Mix together the soaked bread and all the remaining ingredients in a bowl. Shape the mixture into small balls. Place the balls in the prepared baking dish. Cover with foil and bake for about 20 minutes. Serve with Apple Chutney.

Asian Sesame Chicken Skewers

You can make the marinade and trim the chicken a day ahead. Cook just before serving. This goes great with the Thai Peanut Sauce recipe earlier in this chapter.

Ingredients
24–30 (6-inch) wooden skewers
½ cup canned low-sodium chicken stock
¼ cup chopped fresh cilantro, plus extra for garnish
2 tablespoons tamari or low-sodium soy sauce
2 tablespoons sesame oil
2 garlic cloves, minced
4–5 drops (or to taste) hot sauce
1½ pounds boneless, skinless chicken breasts (about 6 halves)
Black sesame seeds, for garnish (about 2 tablespoons)

Directions
Place the wooden skewers in a tall glass of water to soak for at least 15 minutes while preparing the chicken. (This will help prevent them from burning under the broiler.)

To make the marinade, combine the stock, cilantro, tamari, sesame oil, garlic, and hot sauce in a medium-size bowl; whisk until blended. Rinse the chicken under cold running water and pat dry with paper towels. Cut the chicken into ½-inch-wide strips the length of the breast. You should have about 18 to 24 strips. (The strips will vary somewhat in size.) Add the chicken strips to the marinade, cover, and refrigerate for 15 minutes.

Just before preparing to serve, lightly oil a broiler rack and position it about 4 inches from the heat source. Preheat oven broiler to medium.

Remove the chicken strips from the marinade and discard the marinade. Thread one strip on a presoaked wooden skewer. Thread the remaining chicken on the remaining skewers. (Threading the strips in the form of an S will help them stay on the skewer.)

Place the skewers on the broiler rack and broil for about 3 minutes. Turn the skewers over and broil for another 3 to 4 minutes, until the chicken is no longer pink. Remove from the oven and sprinkle with sesame seeds and chopped cilantro. Serve hot.

Beef Tenderloin Bites with Creamy Horseradish Sauce

This is a delicious and impressive appetizer — well worth the cost. The horseradish sauce can be made a day or two in advance and kept refrigerated.

Ingredients
¼ cup prepared horseradish
½ cup low-fat or fat-free sour cream or nonfat yogurt
2 (6-ounce) filet mignon steaks
1½ tablespoons olive oil
¼ teaspoon kosher salt
Freshly cracked black pepper, to taste
12 Asian soup spoons
12 toothpicks
Chopped fresh parsley, for garnish

Directions
In a small bowl, mix together the horseradish and sour cream. Set aside.

Cut each steak into 6 cubes as evenly sized as possible. Transfer to a medium-size bowl and toss with 1 tablespoon of the olive oil, salt, and pepper until evenly coated.

Heat the remaining ½ tablespoon of olive oil in a nonstick sauté pan over medium-high heat. When very hot, but not smoking, add the beef cubes and sear on each side for about 1 minute per side for rare, about 1½ minutes per side for medium.

Transfer the meat to a plate and tent with tinfoil to keep warm. Let rest for about 7 minutes to allow the juices to reabsorb.

To serve, arrange the spoons on a serving platter. Use a toothpick to spear a piece of meat and place it on one of the spoons; continue with the remaining pieces. Drizzle any remaining beef juices over each piece. Add a dollop of the horseradish sauce just to the side of each piece of beef. Garnish with the chopped parsley and serve warm.

Groovy Guacamole

A favorite party appetizer with a major healthy punch. Inflammation will stay away from any party serving this as an appetizer.

Ingredients
2 large ripe avocados, coarsely chopped
1 small white onion, diced
1 tomato, unpeeled and diced
1 jalapeño pepper, thinly sliced
Juice of 1 lime
Salt, to taste

Directions
Gently combine all the ingredients in a serving bowl and serve as a salad or dip for whole-grain tortilla chips.

Fresh Pepper Salsa

Tomatoes are a great source of the antioxidant vitamin C, but are also classified as a nightshade vegetable. Try this salsa without worrying about inflammation. You can also get creative and make your salsa with other vegetables, fruits, and spices.

Ingredients

1 yellow bell pepper

1 orange bell pepper

1 or 2 poblano chilies

2 Anaheim chilies

1 or 2 jalapeño peppers

2 cloves garlic

¼ of a red onion

Juice of ½ lime

Directions

Freshly crushed black pepper, to taste Canola oil (enough to coat the pan) Cilantro, chopped, to taste (optional)

Place all ingredients (except the oil) in a food processor and pulse until desired chunkiness results. Taste and adjust for saltiness and heat.

In a medium pot, heat oil until slightly smoking. Add blended pepper mixture. Cook on high for 8 to 10 minutes, stirring occasionally. Sprinkle some chopped cilantro on top, if desired. Serve hot, cold, or at room temperature with tortilla chips, as a garnish for fish or poultry, or in your favorite burrito.

Traditional Hummus

Hummus is a popular dish throughout the Middle East and Mediterranean. It is a great source of iron and vitamin C, making it ideal for vegetarians, especially vegans. It also offers plenty of protein, fiber, and healthy monounsaturated fats.

Ingredients

1 lemon
¼ bunch fresh parsley
1 cup chickpeas (or other type of white bean), cooked
½ bulb roasted garlic
2 teaspoons extra-virgin olive oil
1 to 2 tablespoons tahini paste
Freshly cracked black pepper, to taste Kosher salt or sea salt, to taste (optional)
Zest and juice the lemon. Chop the parsley.

Directions
In a blender, purée the cooked chickpeas, then add the garlic, lemon zest, and juice. Continue to purée until the mixture is thoroughly combined. Drizzle in the olive oil in a stream while continuing to purée until all the oil is incorporated and the mixture is smooth. Remove the mixture from the blender and season with salt and pepper. Adjust seasonings to taste. Before serving, sprinkle with chopped parsley.

Fava Bean Hummus with Tahini and Pistachios

If you need extra liquid to help purée the fava beans, you may add olive oil or a splash of vegetable broth, but don't overdo it. The hummus should be thick, not runny. Serve this with toasted pita pieces or bagel chips or with fresh vegetables for dunking.

Ingredients
1 (15-ounce) can fava beans, drained and rinsed
3 cloves garlic, or to taste
Juice from 1 lemon, or more to taste
3 tablespoons olive oil, or more as needed to process
1 to 2 tablespoons tahini paste
Salt and freshly ground black pepper, to taste
½ cup minced parsley

¾ cup toasted pistachios

Directions
Put the beans, garlic, lemon juice, olive oil, tahini, salt, and pepper into a food processor or blender and purée.
Spoon the mixture into a bowl and stir in the parsley and pistachios.
Chill until serving time.

Avocado Cumin Dip

The unique flavor of cumin complements the avocado without being overbearing. This dip is perfect with a south-of-the-border menu or spread on warm tortilla chips.

Ingredients
2 medium-size ripe avocados
2 tablespoons fresh lemon juice
2 tablespoons extra-virgin olive oil
1/8 teaspoon garlic powder
1 tablespoon chives
1 teaspoon sea salt
1 teaspoon ground cumin
Dash of hot sauce
Directions
Peel and seed the avocados; in a medium-size bowl mash the meat until smooth.
Add remaining ingredients; mix to combine thoroughly.
Cover and keep in the refrigerator until ready to serve. Letting this dip sit for 15 minutes helps to blend the flavors.

Curry-Cayenne Peanuts

The key to success for this recipe is a premium-quality curry powder and freshly shelled unsalted peanuts.

Ingredients
1 large egg white
2 tablespoons curry powder
1½ teaspoons kosher salt
Sugar substitute equal to 1 teaspoon granulated sugar
¼ teaspoon cayenne pepper
3 cups unsalted peanuts, shelled

Directions
Preheat oven to 300°F.
Line 2 baking sheets with parchment paper and set aside.
In a medium-size bowl, whip the egg white until frothy. Add the curry powder, salt, sugar substitute, and cayenne pepper; whisk until evenly blended. Add the peanuts and stir until evenly coated.
Spread the nuts in a single layer on the prepared baking sheets. Roast, uncovered, for about 20 minutes until the nuts are dry and toasted. Stir and turn the nuts at least 2 times during the roasting process. (Be very watchful during the last half of baking, as the nuts can burn quickly.) Remove the nuts from the oven and transfer them to a sheet of parchment paper to cool.

Hot Crabmeat Dip

Canned crabmeat works better than fresh crabmeat for this dish. Serve as a dip with raw vegetables and whole-wheat crackers.

Ingredients
8 ounces low-fat or fat-free cream cheese, at room temperature
7½ ounces canned crabmeat
2 tablespoons finely chopped yellow onion
2 tablespoons low-fat milk
1 teaspoon prepared horseradish
1 teaspoon seasoned salt

Freshly cracked black pepper, to taste
1/3 cup sliced almonds
Directions
Preheat oven to 375°F.
Combine the cream cheese, crabmeat, onion, milk, horseradish, salt, and pepper in a medium-size bowl; mix until well blended.
Transfer the crabmeat mixture to a 9-inch pie plate or ovenproof dish and sprinkle with the sliced almonds. Bake uncovered for 15 minutes until hot and bubbly. Serve hot.

Spicy Roasted Chickpeas

Spicy roasted chickpeas provide a nice dose of fiber and protein without the fat and calories of regular nuts and seeds.

Ingredients
2 tablespoons olive oil
½ teaspoon each ground coriander, ground cumin, and red pepper flakes
¼ teaspoon seasoned salt
2 cups canned chickpeas, rinsed and drained

Directions
Preheat oven to 400°F. Spray a nonstick baking sheet with nonstick spray and set aside.
Combine the oil and seasonings together in a mediumsize bowl. Add the chickpeas and toss until evenly coated. Spread out the beans in a single layer on the prepared baking sheet and place in the oven. Shake the pan every 10 minutes to make sure the beans are cooking evenly. Bake for 20 to 30 minutes, until crisp and golden. Let cool slightly before serving. Can be made the day before and kept in an airtight container.

Fruit-Stuffed French Toast

The eggy flavor of challah creates the rich profile of this dish. If you never stray from whole grains, replace the challah with 100 percent whole-wheat bread.

Ingredients

½ teaspoon olive oil
3 small to medium loaves challah bread
1 pint seasonal fresh fruit
2 whole eggs or ½ cup egg substitute
4 egg whites
¼ cup skim milk
1 cup orange juice
¼ cup nonfat plain yogurt
¼ cup confectioners' sugar

Directions

Preheat oven to 375°F. Grease a baking sheet with the oil.

Slice the bread into thick (2½- to 3-inch) slices with a serrated knife at a severe angle to form long bias slices (a medium-large loaf of challah will yield 3 thick bias slices). Cut a slit into the bottom crust to form a pocket.

Peel the fruit if necessary, then dice into large pieces and fill the pockets in the bread. Press the pocket closed.

In a large mixing bowl, beat the eggs and egg whites, then add the milk. Dip the bread into the egg mixture, letting it fully absorb the mixture. Place the bread on the prepared baking sheet. Bake for 10 minutes on one side, flip, and bake 10 minutes more.

While the bread is baking, pour the orange juice in small saucepan; boil until reduced by half and the mixture becomes syrupy. Remove the French toast from the oven, and cut in half diagonally. Serve each with dollop of yogurt, a drizzle of juice, and a sprinkling of sugar.

Blackberry Buckwheat Flapjacks

The seeds of blackberries are a good source of fiber, omega-3 fatty acids, and protein. These berries are available to enjoy fresh and frozen all year round.

Ingredients
½ cup all-purpose flour
½ cup 100% whole-wheat flour
½ cup buckwheat flour
3 tablespoons sugar
1½ teaspoons baking powder
1 teaspoon baking soda
½ teaspoon salt
2 eggs or ½ cup egg substitute
3 tablespoons melted butter
1½ cups buttermilk
1 cup blackberries

Directions
Whisk together the three flours, sugar, baking powder, baking soda, and salt in a large bowl.
Whisk together eggs, melted butter, and buttermilk in another bowl.
Stir egg mixture into the flour mixture until combined. There will be lumps; be careful not to over-mix.
Pour about 1/3 cup batter for each pancake onto a hot oiled griddle or pan. Scatter several blackberries on top of batter. Flip pancake when bubbles have formed and started to pop through the batter. Cook on other side for a minute.
Serve hot with maple syrup.

Crepes with Blueberry Sauce

This crepe recipe can be used with roasted vegetables and Walnut-Parsley Pesto (Chapter 17), or with other cooked vegetables and topped with grated Romano cheese.

Ingredients
Crepes
4 eggs
1 cup soy or rice milk
½ cup water
½ teaspoon sea salt
1 cup spelt flour
3 tablespoons melted butter

Apple-Blueberry Filling
1 apple
1 pear
1 teaspoon stevia powder
1 cup water
2 cups blueberries
1 tablespoon cornstarch Cinnamon, to taste (optional)

Directions
Crepe
Combine all crepe ingredients in a blender; purée until smooth. Scrape sides and purée until everything is combined. Place in fridge for at least 2 hours, or overnight.
Heat a crepe pan; spray with oil. When hot, pour ¼ cup batter onto a 10-inch pan (2 tablespoons for a 7-inch pan); swirl around to cover the bottom. Cook until browned on bottom, about 1 minute.
Loosen the crepe with a spatula or knife; flip with your fingers. Cook the second side for about 30 seconds.
Stack the crepes to keep them warm; cover with a clean cloth towel.

Filling
Peel and core the apple and pear; slice and place in a heavy saucepan with sweetener and ½ cup water.
Add the blueberries; bring mixture to a simmer; cook until fruit is tender, about 10 minutes.

Dissolve the corn starch in the remaining water; add to the fruit while cooking. Stir until liquid thickens. Remove from heat and set aside. Lay out a crepe on a plate; spoon some of the fruit mixture onto one half of the crepe. Fold the crepe over; sprinkle cinnamon on top, if desired.

Banana: Oat Bran Waffles

Use either a standard nonstick waffle iron or a Belgian nonstick one that makes waffles with deep indentations to hold pools of rich maple syrup. This recipe yields 6 Belgian waffle squares, or 3 rectangles, but the yield may differ according to the size of your waffle iron.

Ingredients
2 large eggs or ½ cup egg substitute
1 cup buttermilk
2 very ripe bananas
4 tablespoons melted butter plus extra for serving
½ cup all-purpose flour
½ cup 100% whole-wheat flour
½ cup oat bran
2 teaspoons baking powder
½ teaspoon salt
½ cup crushed pecans
Maple syrup or other fruit syrup for serving

Directions
Preheat the waffle iron. Spray both surfaces with nonstick cooking spray.
Beat together the eggs, buttermilk, bananas, and butter until well blended and smooth. Fold in the flour, oat bran, baking powder, and salt, stirring until just combined and moistened; the batter should be stiff, not runny. Fold in the pecans.

Bake waffles according to the manufacturer's directions. Serve hot with extra butter and maple syrup.

Edamame Omelet

The addition of cheese turns this into a fusion dish; to add more Asian flavors, you might want to stir in some shredded daikon and crushed chilies to taste into the mix.

Ingredients
3 tablespoons olive oil, divided
1 teaspoon minced garlic
1 bunch scallions, trimmed and cut into 1-inch pieces
½ cup shelled edamame
1 tablespoon low-sodium soy sauce, or to taste
3 large eggs or ¾ cup egg substitute
½ cup shredded regular or soy Cheddar cheese
Snips of fresh cilantro, for garnish

Directions
Heat 2 tablespoons oil in a small skillet over medium heat and sauté the garlic and scallion for about 2 minutes. Add the edamame and soy sauce and sauté 1 minute more. Remove from the skillet and set aside.
Heat the remaining 1 tablespoon oil in the same skillet. Beat the eggs until mixed and pour into the hot oil. Scatter the shredded cheese on top. Lift up the edges of the omelet, tipping the skillet back and forth to cook the uncooked eggs. When the top looks firm, sprinkle the scallion mixture over one half of the omelet and fold the other half over top.
Carefully lift the omelet out of the skillet. Divide it in half, sprinkle with the cilantro, and serve.

Almond Mascarpone Dumplings

Mascarpone is Italy's answer to cream cheese, with much more flavor.

Ingredients
1 cup whole-wheat flour
1 cup all-purpose unbleached flour
¼ cup ground almonds
4 egg whites
3 ounces mascarpone cheese
1 teaspoon extra-virgin olive oil
2 teaspoons apple juice
1 tablespoon butter
¼ cup honey

Directions
Sift together both types of flour in a large bowl. Mix in the almonds. In a separate bowl, cream together the egg whites, cheese, oil, and juice on medium speed with an electric mixer.
Combine the flour and egg white mixture with a dough hook on medium speed or by hand until a dough forms.
Boil 1 gallon water in a medium-size saucepot. Take a spoonful of the dough and use a second spoon to push it into the boiling water. Cook until the dumpling floats to the top, about 5 to 10 minutes. You can cook several dumplings at once — just take care not to crowd the pot. Remove with a slotted spoon and drain on paper towels.
Heat a medium-size sauté pan on medium-high heat. Add the butter, then place the dumplings in the pan and cook until light brown. Place on serving plates and drizzle with honey.

Raisin Bran Muffins

A breakfast of a glass of orange juice (with pulp) and a bran muffin is a delicious way to start your day with fiber. The raisins add sweetness and fiber, and you can substitute whole-wheat flour for all-purpose flour to add even more fiber.

Ingredients
1 cup boiling water
2½ cups All-Bran cereal
2½ cups all-purpose flour
2½ teaspoons baking soda
1 teaspoon salt
½ cup vegetable oil
1 cup sugar
2 eggs, beaten
2 cups buttermilk
1½ cups raisins
1 cup bran flakes

Directions
Preheat oven to 400°F. Grease a muffin tin or line it with fluted paper cups. Pour the boiling water over 1 cup All-Bran, and let sit for 10 minutes.
Mix the flour, baking soda, and salt in a mixing bowl and set aside.
Mix the oil into the bran and water mixture, then add the remaining bran, sugar, eggs, and buttermilk.
Add the flour mixture to the bran mixture and mix to combine. Stir in the raisins and bran flakes and fill the muffin cups ¾ full with the batter.
Bake muffins for 20 minutes.

Apple Bread

Moist and full of apples, this bread is a great snack with a piece of Cheddar cheese. You give your family fiber with great flavor coming from the whole-wheat flour and apples.

Ingredients
1 packet yeast
3 tablespoons sugar
11/3 cups warm water
3 tablespoons soft butter
1 teaspoon salt
¼ teaspoon baking powder
1¾ cups all-purpose flour
1¾ cups whole-wheat flour
1 cup peeled, chopped apples
1 tablespoon cinnamon mixed with 1 tablespoon sugar
Directions
Combine yeast, ½ teaspoon sugar, and 1/3 cup water in a bowl. Let sit for 5 minutes.

In a mixing bowl, combine remaining water, butter, remaining sugar, salt, and baking powder. Mix in the all-purpose flour and then the yeast mixture with an electric mixer. Add the whole-wheat flour. Knead with a dough hook for 10 minutes.

Turn dough into an oiled bowl. Cover and let rise in a warm place for 1 to 2 hours until doubled in bulk.

Punch down dough, then roll it into a rectangle. Scatter the apples over the dough and sprinkle them with the cinnamon sugar. Roll into a cylinder and place in an oiled loaf pan. Cover and let it rise in a warm place for 90 minutes until doubled in size.

Preheat oven to 350°F. Uncover bread and bake for 50 minutes.

Conclusion

Take care of yourself and take care of your body with daily practices that will reduce inflammation.

If you or someone you love is dealing with a chronic condition, it is important to work with your physician to develop the best possible treatment plan. Ask your doctor for a referral to a registered dietitian to receive a nutrition treatment plan designed specifically for you and that works with your personal needs and preferences.

People in the Mediterranean region have been enjoying this type of food plan for centuries thanks to the flavors, variety, and nourishment it offers. There's also a reason why it's currently viewed as one of the best diets for overall health: It relies on foods known to reduce the risk of heart disease, obesity, and type 2 diabetes all while improving mood, cognition, and life expectancy.

The key to sticking to the Mediterranean diet is to view it as a lifestyle rather than a quick fix or strict meal plan. Remember that you don't have to give up any one food entirely Instead, try adopting the principles of the diet to fit your individual needs and food preferences.

Printed in Great Britain
by Amazon

46342870R00064